Gentle Giants

Cindy Rodriquez
Jo Cleland

Rourke
Publishing LLC
Vero Beach, Florida 32964

www.rourkepublishing.com

PHOTO CREDITS: © Martina Berg: Cover; © Ryan Poling: Title Page; © Chen Fu Soh, © totallyjamie: Illustrations; © kevdog: page 5, 7; © Donald Gargano: page 9, © Gary Martin: page 11; © Heike Mirabella: page 13; © Sharon Morris: page 15; © Hans Meerbeek: page 17; © Yoka Van Eekelen: page 19; © Eric Gevaert: page 21

Editor: Kelli Hicks

Cover and Interior design by: Heather Botto

Library of Congress Cataloging-in-Publication Data

Rodriguez, Cindy.
  Gentle giants / Cindy Rodriguez and Jo Cleland.
    p. cm. -- (My first science library)
  ISBN 978-1-60472-542-1
  1. Gorilla--Juvenile literature. I. Cleland, Joann. II. Title.
  QL737.P96R64 2009
  599.884--dc22
                                        2008027363

Printed in the USA

CG/CG

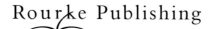

Rourke Publishing

www.rourkepublishing.com – rourke@rourkepublishing.com
Post Office Box 3328, Vero Beach, FL 32964

Gorillas are...

flat-nosed apes.
Their nostrils
open wide.

Gorillas are...

careful watchers with
tiny, beady eyes.

4

Gorillas are...

hairy apes.
Old males have
silver backs.

Gorillas are...

shy animals.
They hoot to warn
of attacks.

Gorillas are...

plant eaters.
They feast on
leaves and fruits.

Gorillas eat grass, bark, berries, shoots, and roots.

12

13

Gorillas are...

family creatures.
They live in little groups.

Gorillas protect each other in these bands called troops.

17

Gorillas are...

gentle giants.
They tenderly teach
their young.

18

19

Gorillas are...

now endangered.
Take care or
they'll be gone.
Gorillas are amazing apes!

Glossary

males (MALZ): Males are boys. Adult male gorillas can weigh up to 440 pounds (200 kilograms).

nostrils (NOSS-truhlz): Nostrils are the holes in a nose that air goes in and out of. Gorilla's nostrils are large and flat.

shoots (SHOOTZ): The small twigs or branches growing out of trees. When gorillas eat shoots, they sometimes eat the bugs that are on them too!

troops (TROOPZ): Troops are groups of gorillas that live together. Gorillas live in bands of six or seven individuals. A band of gorillas may spend their time grooming each other.

Index

body, 3, 4, 5, 6, 7

food, 10, 11, 12, 13

family, 14, 15, 16, 17, 18, 19

protection, 5, 8, 9, 16, 17, 20

Further Reading

Cleland, Jo. *Gorillas.* Fitzgerald, 2007.

Milton, Joyce. *Gorillas: Gentle Giants of the Forest.* Random House, 1997.

Morozumi, Atsuko. *My Friend Gorilla.* Farrar Straus, 2001.

Rathman, Peggy. *Good Night, Gorilla.* Putnam, 1994.

Thomson, Sarah. *Amazing Gorillas.* HarperCollins, 2006.

Websites

http://www.gorillafund.org/gorilla_fun/for_kids.php

http://kids.nationalgeographic.com/Animals/CreatureFeature/Mountain-gorilla

http://classroomclipart.com/cgi-bin/kids/imageFolio.cgi?direct=Animals/Gorilla

About the Authors

Cindy Rodriguez

Jo Cleland loves to write books, compose songs, and make games. She loves to read, sing, and play games with children.

24